MY EARTHQUAKE PREPAREDNESS GUIDE

Simple Steps to get You, Your Family and Pets Prepared

Be Prepared Not Scared

Jack. Klout

JACKIE KLOOSTERBOER

Editor: Nesta Primeau

Produced by:

FriesenPress
Suite 300 – 852 Fort Street
Victoria, BC, Canada V8W 1H8

www.friesenpress.com

Distributed to the trade by The Ingram Book Company

The information contained in this guidebook is one of many tools
available to help you and your family along the road to preparedness.
During times of disaster always follow the direction of authorities.

Table of Contents

Acknowledgements

This book is truly the result of the efforts of family and friends and the people who have sat through and listened to me speak on Emergency Preparedness. Your questions and comments have helped me identify the information that needs to be available to help get ourselves; our families and our pets prepared for whatever disaster comes our way.

As I am about to submit this book for publication, I have just returned from supporting the evacuees of an apartment, where a fire roared through the building leaving 20 families displaced - some with no home to return to. The irony is – I had presented an emergency preparedness session to these residents a few months back.

Some of the residents had followed my advice and had their Grab and Go Kits in place, while others had done little or nothing to prepare. Those who were prepared were getting through the event so much better as they had plans in place and they had the supplies they needed. Those who were not prepared were struggling trying to figure out what their next move would be to get their lives back on track.

My reason for writing this book is to help you get prepared so when faced with a disaster you will have what you need to get through the event. We know we could be faced with a multitude of disasters such as earthquakes, flooding, hurricanes, house and apartment fires just to name a few. It has been proven time and time again

– people who are prepared get through the event much better than those who are not prepared.

Make sure you get your plans in place, and do it now – before disaster strikes – once the disaster hits it's too late. Your family and pets are counting on you!

Special Thanks to

Nesta Primeau – without your amazing editing this guidebook would still be a Word document sitting on my computer

Brandy DePhillip – your hard work in helping me determine what should and should not be included in this guidebook is greatly appreciated.

My Family and Friends - your continued support and understanding in me writing this book is greatly appreciated. I continually talk about Emergency Preparedness but to put it into words was a challenge – but definitely a worthwhile challenge and I appreciate all your help and support along the way.

Introduction

Living on the West Coast of Canada, we need to understand that our area is vulnerable - at any time we could be impacted by a devastating earthquake. Experts predict it's only a matter of time before the "Big One" hits. So why then, are so few of us prepared to deal with earthquakes?

We saw the challenges residents of Japan and New Zealand faced as they tried to put their lives back together following their earthquakes. British Columbia long overdue for an earthquake had a wake-up call October 29, 2012 when a 7.7-magnitude earthquake struck Haida Gwaii. Communities throughout British Columbia and as far away as Edmonton felt the quake. Fortunately there was minimal damage and no injuries; but the questions being asked now – what would have happened if this had of occurred in the Vancouver area. It would have been devastating.

The time to prepare is now – before the earthquake strikes. Once the earthquake hits it will be too late. Store shelves will be empty, homes and workplaces will be damaged. We may not be able to locate our family members and pets simply because we did not take the necessary steps to prepare. First responders will be overwhelmed; help will not arrive as quickly as usual. The reality is – after an earthquake or any major disaster you could be on your own for 72 hours or longer.

There is no shortage of information on emergency preparedness - Google "Emergency Preparedness" and you will receive about 12,300,000 results. Google "Earthquake Preparedness" and you will find about 1,120,000 results. With this many sites offering ideas, it becomes a daunting task to pinpoint useful information on Earthquake Preparedness.

This is why I have compiled this guidebook. It will help you and your family get prepared. It is condensed into easy to follow steps you can take in advance to ensure your preparedness. If you need additional information on any of the topics addressed, you can search specific websites that provide relevant information.

This guidebook is your family's starting point on your road to emergency preparedness. The time to prepare is now - before disaster strikes. After the earthquake it will be too late.

Hazards in Your Community

To be properly prepared, you need to know what you have to be prepared for. Ask yourself what is likely to happen where you live and work. While the focus of this guidebook is earthquakes, there are a variety of disasters that can impact us all. Following an earthquake there is the possibility of secondary disasters such as fires, floods, explosions, landslides and tsunamis. We need to be aware of aftershocks as these can occur minutes, hours, days or even months after the initial quake. Aftershocks can be just as powerful as the original earthquake.

Imagine the following scenario:

> Jim and Jane and their two children Jeremy and Cody live in a neighbourhood located beside a creek. It's a pleasant area of town with newer homes and many young families.

> To enter their neighbourhood, Jim and Jane must either cross a railroad track or use a small bridge to cross a creek. Either of these routes could be closed following an earthquake. Jim and Jane need to plan in advance how they would access their neighbourhood should the routes they normally rely on be closed to traffic.

They also need to identify other potential sources of danger that could be secondary results of an earthquake. These might include house fires, train derailments, or mud slides. If creek levels rose, Jim and Jane's neighbourhood would likely flood.

Jim and Jane need to consider what would happen if Jim were at work when the earthquake struck. Jim works in the city which is 8 km (5 miles) away. He alternates between taking transit and driving his car to and from his office. Should an earthquake strike, transit may not operate and bridges might be temporarily closed. Traffic will be gridlocked as people desperately try to leave the city. It could be hours before Jim is able to return home.

Jim and Jane need to have a plan in place to ensure that either one of them are able to look after the children on their own. Having a plan in place will alleviate worry.

As they develop their family emergency plan Jim and Jane will consider the following:

- *In addition to his regular route to and from work, Jim needs to identify alternate routes he could use.*

- *Jim's brother Keith lives 2 km (1.2 miles) from Jim's workplace. Keith's home has a spare bedroom. Jim will ask Keith if staying with him temporarily is an option.*

- *8 km (5 miles) is a considerable distance between Jim's home and his workplace, but he could ride his bike that distance or maybe even walk home from work. Before deciding whether to walk or bike, Jim must ensure in advance that he has a bike and helmet, walking or riding shoes and emergency supplies. Jim could arrange with Keith to leave his bike at his house. His "Work Grab and Go Kit" containing walking shoes and emergency supplies would be available at his place of employment. At the outset, Jim would have items he needs to make his way home.*

· *At home, Jane would access supplies in emergency kits the family prepared in advance. After an earthquake, she and the children would follow their family emergency plan to cope with challenges they will face over the hours or days following an earthquake.*

While developing their emergency preparedness plans, Jim and Jane identified challenges they might face and determined how to best respond following the disaster. Their plans laid out several scenarios around where Jim, Jane, Jeremy and Cody might be when an earthquake strikes. Now it's your turn.

TASK #1: Identify hazards that could impact you and your family at home and at work. Put plans in place how you can best respond to them.

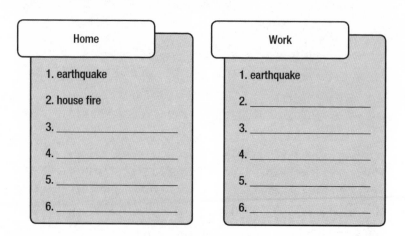

Home

1. earthquake

2. house fire

3. _____

4. _____

5. _____

6. _____

Work

1. earthquake

2. _____

3. _____

4. _____

5. _____

6. _____

Identify routes you could use to return home if your normal route is not useable.

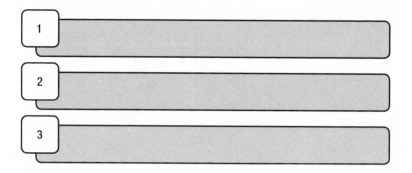

1

2

3

Connecting with your Family

Your first priority following a disaster is to connect with your family. Following major disasters we watch news reports of people searching for their loved ones. There are a number of ways this can be done – but like anything else it needs to be planned before the event takes place.

Family Meeting Places

Establishing "Family Meeting Places" is the first step in reconnecting with your family after an emergency or disaster. Family Meeting Places are pre-identified locations where you and your family will meet if you must evacuate your home or if you are not able to return home.

I know what you are thinking and yes, today almost everyone carries a cell phone. Usually you will be able to contact your family by cell phone, but for the times when you have forgotten your phone, the battery is dead, or the phone can`t be found – worse yet circuits are overloaded or cell phone towers are down – you will be relieved to have back-up plans. Back-up plans are essential.

Family Meeting Place #1 – Evacuating your Home

Imagine a cold dark winter evening. You and your family are at home. The kids are doing their homework upstairs and your partner is in the kitchen making lunches. You are checking emails in your office. All of a sudden an explosion occurs in the basement violently shaking your house. The shrill sound of smoke alarms blasts throughout your house alerting your family of danger. Everyone in your family knows when smoke alarms sound they are to immediately evacuate the house.

Since you are spread throughout your home, everyone is forced to leave through a different door. The fire is blazing and there is no time to locate family members before evacuating. You must get out NOW.

You run outside into the cold dark night and watch in horror as flames shoot through the roof. In the distance you hear sirens of fast approaching fire trucks. But where are your family members?

Panic overtakes you as you run around screaming out their names – you don't know where anyone is. You don't know if everyone has made it out of the house safely.

This is where your Family Meeting Place proves its weight in gold. When you and your family evacuate, each of you will immediately go to your Family Meeting Place. This will quickly identify who has made it out of the home to safety and who may need assistance getting out. If a family member does not arrive at your Family Meeting Place, alert the Fire Department.

When selecting your Family Meeting Place, choose a location that is easily accessible and easy to remember. It could simply be across the street in front of a neighbour's house.

Family Meeting Place #2 – Unable to Return Home

You must now identify your second Family Meeting Place, which should be away from your home but within walking distance. It must be a location familiar to your family - perhaps a friend's house, a restaurant, a park, or a community center.

All family members will report to this location if they are unable to return home, if they are asked by emergency responders to evacuate the home, or if they are unable to connect with each other using cell phones. This slightly more distant Family Meeting Place will provide a quick way of reuniting your family. Once your family is together you can determine your next move.

> *Imagine driving home from work one evening to find your street behind barricades. A police car with lights flashing is parked diagonally, blocking access. The officer informs you that nobody is allowed to enter your street because of a police incident. They are unsure how long it will be until you can return home. The police suggest you make alternate plans for the next four to six hours.*
>
> *Your son is on his way home from soccer practice. Your daughter is at work and will return home in two hours. Your partner will return from work in an hour.*
>
> *When your family arrives to find the police car blocking your road, each family member would immediately try to communicate by phone. If you are able to communicate by phone, that is great. If you cannot communicate by phone the next step is to meet at the pre-determined Family Meeting Place outside your neighbourhood.*

Family Meeting Place #3 – Near Work

Many of us commute long distances to work each day. Sometimes other family members work in the same area. This is a good reason to establish your third Family Meeting Place, a location closer to work rather than in your residential neighbourhood. Once you have met at the pre-identified location, you can decide on your next move.

TASK #2: Follow these steps to ensure you and your family will be able to connect after an emergency or disaster.

1. Select Family Meeting Place #1 - Close to your home. Select a location where you and your family will meet if forced to evacuate your home quickly, perhaps because of a fire. At the lamp post or mailbox across the street or simply across the street from your home will work well.

2. Select Family Meeting Place #2 - Within walking distance of your home. Select a location within walking distance of your home for your Second Family Meeting place. It could be a friend or family member's home or you might decide on a restaurant, park or shopping mall. If you choose a private residence, be sure to inform your friends or relatives of your Family Meeting Place procedure. Ensure that family members know to report to that particular location in the event they are unable to return to home or make telephone contact.

3. Select Family Meeting Place #3 - Close to Work. If you and other family members work in the same area, select a Family Meeting Place close to that location. From this location you will determine your next move. You might decide to walk or bike home, stay downtown or spend the night at a friend's home.

4. Use the chart to list your Family's Meeting Places

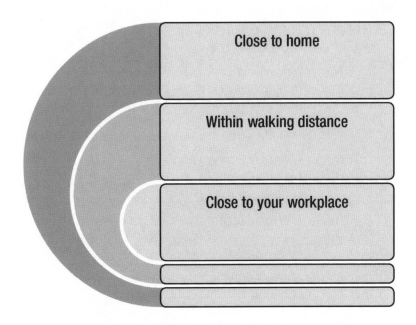

Close to home

Within walking distance

Close to your workplace

Out of Area Contact

In our day-to-day lives we don't think twice about calling our husbands or wives, friends or neighbours to tell them the latest news. We use land lines and cell phones; we text or use Facebook; we tweet. These methods of communicating usually work well – but when an earthquake or a significant event occurs, these means of communication may not be available to us. Then what?

This is where your "Out of Area Contact" comes in. Often overlooked, an Out of Area Contact may be the only way to communicate with your family.

Your Out of Area Contact is a friend or family member who lives out of the province or state. Often, long distance lines work following disasters even when local phone lines are damaged or overloaded.

Using your Out of Area Contact, each family member will contact that person to inform them of their whereabouts. It is important to keep your calls short to give others an opportunity to get through. As each family member phones, they will receive an update on other family members who have already made contact. This may be the only way to connect with your family even if they are only a few minutes away.

> *My family uses our cousin Phil as our Out of Area Contact. Phil lives in Edmonton, out of the danger area for earthquakes that might take place in British Columbia. Each member of my family will contact Phil if we cannot connect with each other using our accustomed means of communication. We will advise him of our situation and condition and receive updates on other family members who have already checked in. If a family member has not yet reached Phil, we will call back later for an update.*

Facebook, Twitter, Texting

During many of the recent disasters around the world we have seen people using their Facebook accounts to connect with family following a disaster. This may be a good option for many but we need to be cautious when using methods other than regular phone lines.

For example, if I were to try connecting with my parents using Facebook it is not going to happen – I would have better luck with carrier pigeons - but using Facebook to connect with my kids is a viable option. Be careful when selecting methods to communicate; ensure that all family members are familiar with the options you choose.

When I present emergency preparedness sessions, the following question is always asked – what about texting and Twitter– will they work after an emergency or disaster?

The simple answer is we do not know in advance what means of communication will function after a major earthquake. We do not know what systems will be impacted until the earthquake has taken place. But we do know that if you have communication options in place before the disaster strikes, you will significantly improve your chances to connect with your family.

TASK #3: **Ensure you have plans in place to connect with your family following an emergency or disaster.**

1. Select a friend or family member who lives out of your province or state to be your Out of Area Contact. Friends or relatives living in Alaska, British Columbia, Washington, Oregon or California are not good choices for an Out of Area Contact as these locations are at risk for earthquakes.

2. Ask your Out of Area Contact if they are willing to take on this role. Make sure they understand what is expected of being your Out of Area Contact.

3. Complete Out of Area Contact Cards available at www.myeqplan.com. Make sure each member of your family carries an Out of Area Contact card with them. It is not uncommon to forget numbers in a disaster situation.

4. Identify other ways of communicating with your family such as Facebook, texting and Twitter. A word of caution - don't assume that because you can send a text, the person you sent it to will receive it. Their phone may or may not be working.

Out of Area Contact
Name:
Home Phone:
Cell Phone:
Email:

Family Photo

A picture is worth a thousand words! Your family photo is an important part of your emergency plan. Keep it in your Grab and Go Kit. Not only will it provide comfort to have a family photo but it can be used to help authorities locate or identify family members if someone becomes lost or separated from the family.

In addition to carrying a group photo of your family, you should have a headshot of each individual family member alone.

If you have pets, take a photo of them as well. It is easier to show a photo of your pet rather than trying to describe what your golden retriever looks like. Take a photo of the pet alone as well as one of your pet with you. Having yourself in the photo with your pet can help prove you are the rightful owner.

TASK #4: Make sure you have photos of your family and pets in your emergency kits.

1. Take a group photo of your family including pets.

2. Take an individual photo of each family member.

3. Take an individual photo of your pet.

4. Along with a printed copy of your photo, its a good idea to keep photos of family and pets on a password protected memory stick should you need more copies.

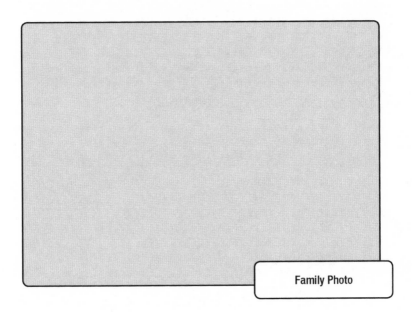

Family Photo

Insert your individual family photos below

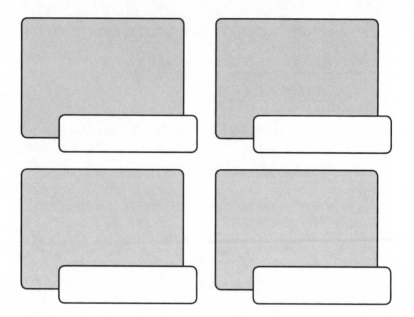

Around the House

When an earthquake strikes, you will be more comfortable staying in your home if this is possible. If your home withstands the earthquake and if you have the necessary supplies on hand, there is a good chance you can stay in your home, rather than sleeping on a gym floor in an evacuation center.

Making your Home Safe

No ifs, ands, or buts - if you live on the West Coast, earthquake preparedness must be at the top of your family's "To Do" list. When it comes to preparing your home for an earthquake, you need to consider conditions both inside and outside your home. You need to identify what you can do to make your home safe for you, your family and your pets.

When an earthquake strikes you will often feel the rocking motion you would experience in a boat on rocky water. With that rocking motion in mind – walk through each room of your home with the checklist provided to identify what you need to do to make sure your home is safe. This is a great starting point to ensure your family and pets will be safe.

Your kitchen is probably the most dangerous room in your home when it comes to earthquakes. Our counters are loaded with microwaves, coffee makers, toasters and TV's. Imagine what will happen when the ground starts moving - all those countertop items could become projectiles shooting across the room, potentially causing injury.

Kitchen cupboards are an area for concern. We tend to put heavy items like Corning Ware up high and lighter items like Tupperware down low. Simply reversing this and putting your heavy items down low and your lighter items up high can make a big difference. You will be a lot better off hit with a piece of Tupperware rather than a heavy casserole dish.

Think about your large appliances - your refrigerator, stove, dishwasher, washer and dryer. During an earthquake all of these could dance across the room if they are not properly secured. Even worse, what if gas appliances break free causing a rupture in your gas line? Purchasing stoppers or wedges at your hardware or Emergency Preparedness store can keep these appliances in place during an earthquake. Ask your local gas company about using flexible hoses on gas appliances as a safety precaution.

Heavy items like TV stands and bookcases need to be properly secured to studs in your wall - if these topple over they could cause significant damage. Worse yet, they could injure your family or pets if they became caught underneath or between these heavy items. It is also possible that heavy pieces of furniture could block your family's evacuation routes.

Where you place your furniture is another concern. You want to that ensure sofas and beds are not underneath windows or heavy picture frames.

When I moved to Vancouver, I leased a small but trendy Yaletown apartment. My bedroom was so small that I had no choice but to put my bed in front of the window. As an emergency planner, my biggest fear was reading the newspaper headline,

"Emergency Planner injured by broken glass during earthquake". But there was no choice -- the only spot for my bed was underneath the window.

How could I lessen the risk of being injured by broken glass? I purchased a pair of heavy drapes. Was this ideal? No, it was not, but it was significantly better than leaving my bed unprotected in front of a window. Each night when I went to bed I closed my blinds and drew the drapes. If we had the earthquake, I would be better protected from broken glass.

Be sure to keep a pair of running shoes under each person's bed. If there is an earthquake in the middle of the night and the power is out you might need to navigate your escape through broken glass. Having shoes under your bed will help protect your feet.

Outside your home, check your chimney for loose bricks. Inspect your roof for loose tiles or shingles. You will also need to make sure your home is properly secured to the foundation. If you are unsure on how to do this – seek help from a professional.

If you live in an apartment or townhouse, consult with your strata council or building manager. In many strata complexes, there are committee members who oversee emergency preparedness. The committee ensures that residents and structures are prepared for the possibility of an earthquake. Some stratas even go as far as designating volunteer owners to help their neighbours secure hot water tanks or heavy furniture. This is especially helpful for owners not able to perform these tasks themselves.

TASK #5: Use the "Home Hazard Hunt" to ensure your home is prepared for an earthquake. If you are unable to do these tasks yourself hire a reputable contractor.

√	Home Hazard Hunt
	Inspect your chimney for loose bricks and ensure your chimney is securely fastened to the structure to protect against windstorms or earthquakes.
	Inspect your roof for loose tiles or shingles. Ensure your roof is securely attached to the structure of your home to protect against windstorms or earthquakes.
	Inspect the foundation of your home to ensure your home is properly secured to the foundation.
	Check trees in your yard to ensure they will not fall onto your house or vehicle during a windstorm or earthquake.
	Use an approved seismic restraint kit to secure your hot water tank to the frame of your home.
	Check air tight stoves and seals to prevent leakages of carbon monoxide.
	Secure top heavy furniture such as china cabinets, bookshelves and entertainment units to wall studs.
	Move hanging plants and lamps away from windows and into areas where they cannot hit glass if they swing.
	Install latches on bathroom, kitchen and any other cabinet doors to ensure that doors remain closed during an earthquake and items stay within the cabinets.
	Ensure pictures and mirrors are securely fastened to the wall. Do not hang pictures over beds or seating areas.
	Store toxic and caustic solutions where they cannot be knocked over onto your emergency kits.
	Store heavy items such as Corning Ware down low and plastic items up high. There will be less damage to your family or home if a piece of Tupperware flies out of the cupboard rather than a heavier item.

	Ensure heavy appliances (refrigerator, stove, washer, dryer, etc.) are properly secured so they will not break free causing major damage.
	Where possible, clear or secure small appliances on kitchen counters. In an earthquake these items can become projectiles and cause injury or damage to your family or home.
	Secure collectibles and electronic equipment such as TVs and computers to their shelves or cabinets with hook and loop fasteners, double sided tape, putty or protective rails.
	Visit your local Emergency Preparedness or hardware store to purchase the required supplies needed to make your home safe.

Tasks to Complete		*Supplies to Purchase*	
1		1	
2		2	
3		3	
4		4	
5		5	
6		6	
7		7	
8		8	
9		9	
10		10	

Sewage

Sewer lines often become damaged during an earthquake. If this is the case, you will need to construct a temporary toilet. This is not difficult to do. Remove all the water from the bowl of your toilet and line the bowl with two heavy duty plastic bags – one inside the other. Fold the bags down over the sides of your toilet bowl. Put absorbent material such as kitty litter or shredded newspaper into the inner bag. Defecate directly into the inner bag. Use toilet paper sparingly and put it into the bag. Do not urinate into this bag as urine may cause the bags to deteriorate.

Solid waste is a source of many bacteria-causing diseases (like cholera); it must be disinfected and disposed of properly. Tie the bag loosely when it is half full to allow it to dry out. Label the bag, "Human Waste" then store it in a tightly covered garbage can away from your living areas.

Disinfectants must be added to the waste to help prevent the spread of disease. Use the following as disinfectants:

· Portable toilet chemicals

· Household chlorine bleach

· Hydrated lime. Hydrated lime reduces odor, fights bacteria and dries out waste for easier disposal. Wear a dust mask and rubber gloves when using hydrated lime and always follow the directions. Be careful as it can cause skin irritation and dryness. You can purchase hydrated lime at most nurseries and gardening supply stores.

For urine, use a sturdy bucket or small trash can with a tight fitting lid. A portable camping toilet will work just as well. Line the container with two heavy duty plastic bags. Unlike solid waste, liquid waste is not considered a serious health hazard. It can be disposed of in your yard if emptied in an area away from water supplies such as springs, wells, or areas subject to flooding.

Pour urine into a hole 45–60 cm (18-24 inches) deep and fill the hole with dirt. Make sure you wash your hands with soap and water or use an antibacterial wipe.

It is important to listen to your radio and follow the instructions of your local authorities as they will likely have specific instructions on disposal of human waste. If you are in an apartment building there may be specific instructions that occupants are to follow. These will likely be posted in common areas.

Utilities

Because we rely on a number of utilities as we go about our daily lives, it is important to know what to do with these utilities when faced with an earthquake or major disaster. Do we turn them off? Or, do we leave them on?

Depending on where you live, you may need to deal with additional utilities not listed below. Always check with your local providers for information specific to that utility during time of emergency or disasters.

Gas Meter

If your home has a gas meter, you must know where the meter is located, how to turn it off and under what circumstances it should be turned off. Most gas companies have websites with information related to your community. Read on-line emergency instructions and make sure you know what to do with your gas meter when a disaster strikes.

The instructions in this section are for information only and should not override directions provided by your local utility or Gas Company.

When natural gas is leaked outdoors it rises and dissipates into the atmosphere. But when gas is leaked into a confined space like your home, it can be dangerous. An odorant has been added to natural gas by the manufacturer making it smell like rotten eggs or sulphur, so you can detect a gas leak. Gas can also form a combustible mixture and if ignited by sparks from electrical switches, appliance pilot lights or open flames, an explosion or fire can occur. **If you smell gas you need to get out of your house immediately.**

Just because an earthquake has occurred, you do not necessarily have to turn off the gas. This is important because once you turn off your gas meter, you cannot turn it back on - it must be turned on only by a registered gas contractor. Imagine the wait time to have your gas turned back on if everyone in the neighbourhood turned off the gas to their homes unnecessarily.

The time to shut off your gas is when you hear the hissing noise that leaking gas makes or smell the distinct smell of rotten eggs or sulphur. Keep a wrench near your gas meter or in your home kit to ensure it can easily be shut off when required.

Make sure each responsible member of your family knows the location of your gas meter, where the shut off valve is located, where the wrench is located and how and when to turn off the gas. If you have tenants, it is important they also have this information. Keep a clear path to your gas meter to ensure it can be turned off quickly.

If you live in an apartment building you will not likely have a gas meter for your individual unit – usually there is one gas meter for the building. In townhouse complexes there may be a cluster of gas meters. Ensure someone such as the building manager, custodian, or strata manager knows the process for turning off the gas in your building.

For more information on your gas meter, check with your local gas company. There are excellent websites with information related to your locality. Make sure you follow instructions provided by your gas company.

Hot Water Tank

The rocking or shaking movement of an earthquake could easily cause your hot water tank to topple over causing a flood or worse yet, a break in the gas supply line. When preparing your home to withstand an earthquake, ensure that your hot water tank is properly secured.

Secure your hot water tank using an approved seismic restraint kit designed specifically for this purpose. Ensure it is strong enough for the size of your hot water tank. Hot water tanks can vary in weight so you need to be sure the strapping you use is strong enough to handle the weight of the hot water tank.

Strap the tank in two locations, one strap around the upper third of the tank and the other around the lower third. The lower strap must be at least 101.6mm (4 inches) above the gas controls on the tank. Ensure the strapping is attached to the frame of your house with steel screws or lag bolts - plasterboard anchors are not strong enough to hold your hot water tank. By purchasing an approved kit you will ensure you have reliable parts that have been tested for this purpose. If you are unable to secure the hot water tank yourself, hire a reputable contractor who has experience performing this task.

Electrical Breaker Panel

I am continually amazed at how many people do not know where their main electrical or breaker panel is located in their homes or how to turn them off. This panel controls the main power supply to your home. Learn where it is in case the power to your house needs to be turned off.

When evacuating your home, you do not always have to shut off your electrical panel, but it is recommended you unplug all appliances.

If the power to your home is out, utility companies suggest that you leave an indoor and outdoor light turned on so hydro crews can quickly learn if the power is on or off.

Having power surge cords for your computer can protect your data. These cords are available at computer and hardware stores. When purchasing them ensure they are Canadian Standards Association (CSA) approved.

Water Shut Off

Following an earthquake, there could be breaks in the water lines throughout your community. You must know where your main water shut off is located in your home. Shutting off your water supply could save your home and property from serious flooding and also help keep contaminated water from entering your home should there be damage to the water system. Always listen to authorities and take their direction on handling your utilities.

Downed Power Lines

If you are outside after an earthquake, check for downed power lines. Never take chances with power lines. If you notice a downed power line, stay back and keep others back at least 10 meters (33 feet). Always assume a downed power line is a live power line.

TASK #6: Ensure all responsible family members are familiar with your homes utilities.

1. Gas meter - Ensure you and your family members know how and when to turn off the gas. Keep a wrench in your home kit or near your gas meter. Keep the area around your gas meter clear.

2. Hot water tank - Ensure your hot water tank is securely strapped in place. If it is not, hire a contractor to perform this task or purchase the required supplies from a hardware store and do it yourself.

3. Electrical breaker panel - Ensure each family member knows where the electrical panel is located and how and when to turn it off.

4. Water shut off - Ensure each family member knows when and how to turn off the water supply.

5. Attach instructions to each utility in your home listing when and how to turn off the utility and the proper method for shutting off. This will ensure that correct procedures are followed during a disaster when you may not be able to think clearly.

6. Review these procedures with all responsible family members and tenants within your home.

Smoke Alarms

When responding to fires, I am constantly amazed to find people standing on the street who have just lost absolutely everything they owned to a fire simply because they did not have a working smoke alarm.

Recently, I responded to a house fire. The mom had taken the batteries out of her smoke alarm because every time she cooked, the smoke alarm would go off. Usually she remembered to replace the batteries after cooking, but the one time she forgot, there was a kitchen fire in the middle of the night. Fortunately, their dog woke them up and the mother and her two young children were able to leave the house safely. This family was fortunate to get out unharmed and alive, but if they had a working smoke alarm there would have been significantly less damage to their home.

Smoke alarms **DO** save lives if they are working properly. They also protect your property. Make sure your smoke alarms are Canadian Standards Association (CSA) approved and that you have at least one smoke alarm on each level of your home. Ensure the batteries are changed regularly. It is important that you test your smoke alarms monthly. Refer to the smoke alarm manufacturer's instructions on how to test your alarm.

It is good practice to sleep with your bedrooms doors closed at night. This can help protect your family from a quickly spreading fire.

Carbon Monoxide (CO2) Alarms

Space heaters, water heaters, blocked chimneys and cars running in enclosed spaces can cause carbon monoxide to build up. Carbon monoxide is a colourless and odorless gas, highly flammable, and extremely toxic if inhaled. Symptoms of carbon monoxide poisoning can range from vertigo to toxicity of the central nervous system. To protect your family, you should have a Carbon Monoxide alarm with CSA approval installed in your home. This alarm will warn your family if carbon monoxide levels become dangerous.

Test your Carbon Monoxide alarm monthly and replace the batteries often.

Fire Extinguishers

Your fire extinguisher will not be much use to you or your family if you do not know how to use it or if it has passed the expiry date. We tend to buy fire extinguishers and then put them away in a closet. Because we have not used the fire extinguisher, we forget about it until we are faced with a fire.

When purchasing a fire extinguisher make sure you choose an "A-B-C" fire extinguisher. A-B-C means they can be used on different types of fires. You need to also check to ensure they display the seal of an independent testing laboratory.

Make sure you know how to use the fire extinguisher before a fire begins. Always ensure you have a way out of your house. Instructions for use are on the cylinder, but when facing a fire you will not have time to read the directions. 'PASS' is a helpful acronym to remember:

P: Pull the pin

A: Aim at the base of the fire

S: Squeeze the trigger

S: Sweep side to side

Fire extinguishers come in different sizes. A portable fire extinguisher may be fully discharged in as few as eight seconds. If you have a large fire, do not try to use a fire extinguisher as you may put yourself in danger. Just get out of the house and call 911.

Many local fire departments offer courses in how to use a fire extinguisher. This can be a valuable course for you and members of your family.

TASK #7: Make sure all family members are familiar with the location of alarms and fire extinguishers.

1. Smoke Alarms - Ensure you have a working smoke alarm on each level of your home; test smoke alarms monthly and replace the batteries often.

2. Carbon Monoxide Alarms - Purchase a carbon monoxide alarm and install it immediately. Test your carbon monoxide alarm monthly and replace the batteries often.

3. Fire Extinguisher - Check the expiry date on your fire extinguisher and ensure you know how to use it properly. Ask your local fire department if they offer courses on how to use a fire extinguisher. If they do, register you and your family members.

Emergency Kits

The key to surviving an earthquake or any type of disaster is having the supplies you and your family will need before the disaster takes place. Once the disaster happens – it's too late to be thinking about the supplies you will need.

Emergency kits are your family's life preservers when disaster strikes. Growing up, swimming lessons were a huge part of my life. One of the first things I learned was this: when someone is drowning throw them a life preserver to help save their life.

The point is, to save or improve the quality of your life after an emergency or disaster, you not only need to know what to do, but you must also have the supplies that you will need to do it. This brings us to your "Family's Emergency Kits".

Because we all lead busy lives, your eyes are probably rolling back in your head as you think about the five emergency kits you need to put together to protect you and your family. (It's actually six but pets are covered in another section.) These kits will be your family's life preservers - when disaster strikes the contents of your kits could ensure your family's safety and survival.

1. Grab and Go Kit
2. Home Kit
3. Car Kit
4. Work Kit
5. First Aid Kit

I will discuss each of the kits and explain how they will work for you and your family after an emergency or disaster. You will find a complete list of items required to stock each of the kits following the explanation of the kit. You may already have many of the items you need to include in your kits, so it will be just be a matter of gathering what you have and purchasing what you do not have.

Get busy and get your family's emergency kits in place. The time to do this is now – before disaster strikes.

Grab and Go Kit

It's 3 a.m. and you awake to the sound of pounding on your front door. You bolt upright in bed and try to pull yourself together. You spring out of bed and in the distance you hear the wailing of sirens. You look outside to see red and blue flashing police car lights lining your street. You watch as the police bang on your neighbours' doors. Your heart sinks. You know your worst fears are coming true. You stumble down the stairs with Rupert, your dog, close behind you. As you open the front door the officer advises – "You have ten minutes to evacuate your home. The forest fire is getting closer by the minute".

With Rupert still at your heels, you rush to wake your family so you can lead them to safety. But what about the "stuff" you and your family will need? What about clothes and medications? What about Rupert the dog and Smudge the cat? What will your pets need?

You do not have time to gather all this together now – you have just ten minutes to evacuate.

Think how different this situation would be had you taken the time to put together Grab and Go Kits in advance. Everyone would have the items they need in their kit and would be ready to evacuate at a moment's notice.

Each family member must have a Grab and Go Kit designed to meet their specific needs. If you are a family of four, then you will have four Grab and Go Kits. If you try to put four people's supplies into one kit, the kit will be too heavy to manage. If for some reason you are separated from other family members, someone could be left without their emergency supplies. Always have a kit for each family member.

To begin, choose a bag that is sturdy and easy to carry because you do not know how far you will need to travel. A backpack or a gym bag that you can throw over your shoulder works well. When the kit is assembled it must be light enough to be carried by the person who will use the kit. A suitcase with wheels is not an option.

> *Imagine, 3 a.m. in the pitch black trying to roll your suitcase across a grassy park or down the emergency stairway in your apartment building -- believe me, this would not work well for you.*

The million dollar question is - where do I store my family's Grab and Go Kits? I believe the best location is near the door you will most likely use to evacuate your home. In most cases, this will be the front door. A closet near your front door is the ideal location to store your kits. Ensure your kits do not become buried in your closet as you must have easy access to grab them.

When evacuating, grab as many kits as you can manage. If you are not able to access the area of your home where the Grab and Go Kits are located, don't put yourself in danger – simply get out of your house to safety. Safety is always your first priority.

A word of caution: If you use your garage as the main exit from your house and there is a power outage, garage doors equipped with electric openers may not operate. This is something you need to consider when determining the best location to store your Grab and Go Kits.

I am often asked, "What is the point of putting together Grab and Go Kits for my family if I may not be able to get to them?" I always respond with this question – "What if you could grab your Grab and Go Kit but you do not have a kit to grab? Wouldn't that be worse?"

In a disaster, you will still need your medications. You may not have access to a drug store or even a hospital to replenish medications once you have been evacuated. It is crucial to have your medications in your Grab and Go Kit. Always check with your family doctor or pharmacist before storing medications. You do not want to put yourself in danger using improperly stored medications.

> *I am a diabetic and it is essential that insulin be kept in the refrigerator. I keep all the peripheral pieces such as syringes, pump supplies, alcohol swabs and testing supplies in my Grab and Go Kit. For me it is one extra step to the fridge to grab the insulin if I am evacuated. This saves considerable time as I am not fumbling around for all my supplies.*

We all rely on bank machines to access cash, but if you are anything like me, you don't have cash lying around. Keep cash for emergencies in your Grab and Go Kit. A word of warning that I learned the hard way: if you have children do not tell them there is cash in the Grab and Go Kit – it may not be there when you need it.

You need to have copies of your identification and other important documents such as insurance papers in your Grab and Go Kit. Some people prefer to use a password protected memory stick with all their information stored on it rather than make paper photocopies of their identification. With a memory stick however, you may not have immediate access to your information. Do not assume that when evacuating you will leave with your purse or wallet – often they are forgotten or you do not have time to grab them. But if it is safe to do so, grab your Grab and Go Kit on your way out the door.

When evacuating your home, the last thing on your mind will be your keys. When I respond to house and apartment fires, I often see people standing on the street with their cars parked beside them. They have friends or family to stay with, but have no way of driving to their home because they left their keys behind. The simple remedy to this predicament is to put a set of house and car keys in your Grab and Go Kit.

TASK #8: Prepare a Grab and Go Kit for each family member

1. Use checklists provided to determine what you already have and what you need to purchase to complete your family's Grab and Go Kits. Remember one kit per person.

2. Talk to your family doctor or pharmacist about medications family members regularly take and identity the proper way to store those medications in your Grab and Go Kits.

3. Photocopy your identification and important papers or put on a password protected memory stick.

4. Keep your kits in the closet near the door you are likely to use to evacuate your home.

5. Keep a content list of the supplies you have in your kit along with expiry dates. Review this list twice a year when the clocks change. Ensure all contents are still relevant to the person who belongs to the kit. Make sure that items have not expired.

Grab and Go Kit Check List - Adult

Your Grab and Go Kit is what you will grab and go with when you are evacuated from your home. Everyone in your family, including your pets, must have their own Grab and Go Kit with items necessary for their personal well-being. Remember – it is a kit to grab and go with. Keep heavy items out of the kit.

☐ Food (granola bars, fruit snacks, trail mix)

☐ Water (bottled)

☐ Flashlight and batteries

☐ Radio and batteries

☐ Work gloves

☐ Multi-purpose tool

☐ Dust mask

☐ First Aid Kit with manual

☐ Pain relief, cough and allergy medications

☐ Medications (talk with your family doctor or pharmacist before storing any medications)

☐ Hygiene items (toothbrush, toothpaste, deodorant)

☐ Spare eyeglasses

☐ Contact lens solution

☐ Antibacterial wipes

☐ Change of clothes

☐ Poncho or rain jacket

☐ Walking shoes

☐ Emergency blanket

☐ Book/magazine

☐ Note pad and pen

☐ Spare cell phone

☐ Cell phone charger, lap top charger

☐ Important documents (photocopied or on a memory stick)

☐ Money

☐ Out of Area Contact Card (Completed)

☐ Copy or your Family Emergency Plan

☐ Other items you may require

Grab and Go Kit Check List - Teenagers

Use items from the Adult List then add items specific to your teen-ager's needs. Some items to consider include:

- [ ] Games / Music
- [ ] Comfort Items
- [ ] Book
- [ ] Other items your teenage may require

Grab and Go Kit Check List - Child

Use items from the Adult List then add items specific to your child's needs. Some items to consider include:

- [ ] Games (batteries)
- [ ] Books
- [ ] Crayons/colouring book
- [ ] Small toys
- [ ] Stuffed animal or doll
- [ ] Comfort Items
- [ ] Other items your child may require

Grab and Go Kit Check List - Infants

Use items from the Adult List then add items specific to your infant's needs. Some items to consider include:

- [ ] Diapers
- [ ] Formula
- [ ] Baby food
- [ ] Wipes
- [ ] Receiving blanket
- [ ] Creams/lotions
- [ ] Other items your infant may require

Home Kit

With your family's Grab and Go Kits easily accessible in the front door closet, it is time to move on to the next kit you and your family will need - your Home Kit. Your Home Kit will contain items you and your family will need to stay at home and survive.

Just because there has been an earthquake does not mean you will have to evacuate - you may be able to stay in your home. While you may not have all the comforts you rely on such as electricity and water, if you take steps to prepare your home in case of an earthquake and create your Home Kit, you and your family may be just fine staying home.

Following a widespread disaster, evacuation centers will open, but they certainly will not open within the first few hours. It could take up to 72 hours before they are inspected for safety and opened to the public after an earthquake. Before going to an evacuation centers ask yourself this question: "Do you and your family really want to sleep on a squeaky cot in a gym amongst hundreds of your new best friends?" I am guessing the answer is a resounding "NO!" With a Home Kit in place you increase your chances of being able to stay at home and survive because you will have the supplies you need.

If you are a camper, you will already have many items you need for your Home Kit. It is just a matter of getting them together in one location. A list of items to put in your Home Kit is provided at the end of this section.

Rubbermaid-type bins work well to hold emergency supplies. They are strong and durable and will keep your supplies dry. Using a Rubbermaid-type bin ensures your emergency supplies will be in one convenient location and not scattered around your home. Avoid using cardboard boxes for your Home Kit supplies - over time cardboard may break down. If cardboard boxes become damp, they may become moldy and contaminate your supplies. Cardboard boxes can be awkward to carry.

If you plan to store your Home Kit in the garage, make sure you do not store near chemicals such as weed killers or solvents. If chemical containers topple and land on your kit, supplies will be compromised.

Ensure you have easy access to your Home Kit. Do not let your kits become buried over time. You want to make sure it is easy for you and family members to access your Home Kit when needed. You do not want to start searching for them amongst other items.

TASK #9: Prepare a Home Kit so you, your family and pets will have the items you will need to stay and survive at home.

1. Use Rubbermaid-type bins to store your family's home emergency kit; stock it with items you and your family will need.

2. Use the following checklist to determine what items you already have and what items you need to purchase for your Home Kit.

3. Find a safe location to store your kit. Make sure it is away from chemicals.

4. Ensure you have easy access to your home kit and that it is not buried by other items in your basement or garage.

5. Create a content/inventory list with expiry dates and be sure to check twice a year to ensure all items are still relevant and that none of them have expired.

Home Kit Check List

Authorities always say, "Plan to be on your own without help for three days." But everyone has read news reports – often three days is not enough. Plan for a minimum of seven days to ensure your supplies are adequate. Remember, your family is depending on you during these troubled times.

- ☐ Food – canned/dehydrated
- ☐ Water - __ Litres __ Gallons (use chart from the water section in this guidebook)
- ☐ Flashlight and batteries
- ☐ Radio and batteries
- ☐ Utensils and plates
- ☐ Whistle
- ☐ Scissors
- ☐ Work gloves
- ☐ Safety goggles
- ☐ Duct tape
- ☐ Dust mask
- ☐ Multi-purpose tool
- ☐ Basic tools, hammer, pliers, crowbar
- ☐ Wrench for gas meter

- ☐ Medications – check with family doctor or pharmacist
- ☐ Spare glasses
- ☐ Contact lens solutions
- ☐ Hygiene items
- ☐ Blankets or sleeping bags
- ☐ Tent or shelter for outside use if required
- ☐ Change of clothes for each family member
- ☐ Walking shoes
- ☐ Poncho or rain jacket
- ☐ Money
- ☐ Cell phone and charger
- ☐ House and car keys – extra set
- ☐ Identification
- ☐ Important documents (photocopied or on a memory stick)

- ☐ Fuel operated stove (use outside only)
- ☐ Can opener
- ☐ Cooking utensils
- ☐ Heavy duty garbage bags
- ☐ Lime/bleach (sanitation)
- ☐ Bucket with lid (toilet) and plastic bags

- ☐ Out of Area Contact card (completed)
- ☐ Notebook and pencil
- ☐ Books and or cards
- ☐ Copy of your family emergency plan
- ☐ First Aid Kit with manual
- ☐ Any other items your family may need

Car Emergency Kit

Have car will travel. Have car - have Car Kit. Your Car Kit will be a useful resource when you have a breakdown at the side of the road or during emergency events when you might not be able to get to your destination right away.

On a recent trip to Whistler, a landslide was being cleared on the Sea to Sky Highway. The highway was closed for several hours. Everyone sat in their car waiting for the highway to reopen. Fortunately, I had granola bars and water in my Car Kit. There was a family with young children in the car behind me. They did not have any supplies. They were extremely thankful for the granola bars and water I was able to provide from my Car Kit. You can bet now, they too have a Car Kit safely tucked away in the trunk of their car.

TASK #10: Make sure you have a Car Kit located in the trunk of all your vehicles. Don't forget your RV's and boats – they too should carry emergency kits.

1. Account for all family members and pets when putting together your Car Kit.

2. Use the checklist provided to identify what you need to assemble.

3. If you own RVs or boats, prepare a Kit for each of these vehicles.

Car Kit Check List

Some of us spend a lot of time in our cars. It is essential to have the supplies we will need.

☐ Food (granola bars, trail mix, fruit snacks)	☐ Walking shoes and boots
☐ Water (bottled)	☐ Poncho or rain jacket
☐ Flashlight and batteries	☐ Money
☐ Radio and batteries	☐ Windshield washer fluid
☐ Heavy gloves	☐ Jumper cables
☐ Dust mask	☐ Fire extinguisher
☐ Whistle – to attract attention	☐ Tow rope
☐ Candle in a deep can	☐ Ice scraper and snow brush
☐ Matches	☐ Sand, salt or non-clumping cat litter
☐ Compass	☐ Warning lights or road flares

☐ Roadmaps (GPS may or may not be working)

☐ Cell phone & charger

☐ Multi-purpose tool

☐ Duct tape

☐ First Aid Kit with manual

☐ Emergency blanket

☐ Change of clothes

☐ Tools (shovel, axe, hatchet)

☐ Tire pump

☐ Out of Area Contact card (completed)

☐ Identification

☐ Notebook and pencil

☐ Books or cards

☐ Any other items you may require

First Aid Kit

Today, when you call 911, police, fire and ambulance workers respond quickly to your call. But imagine what it could be like after a major earthquake – first responders will be overwhelmed. Roads and bridges may be damaged or closed making it impossible for anyone to respond to your emergency call. This makes it essential to have a First Aid Kit.

You and family members should also have first aid qualifications. Knowing how to treat injuries on the scene could save your life.

Check with your neighbours to find out who is trained in first aid. Do not get excited if you have a doctor or a nurse as a neighbour – it is likely they will respond to the local hospital and be unable to help your family during a disaster.

Following an earthquake, we have no idea what contaminants may pollute the air. If there is significant damage in your community, air-borne contaminants may be hazardous to your health. A simple cut on your finger could turn into something serious if not treated right away. With First Aid supplies, you will be able to treat minor injuries immediately and prevent infection.

Your First Aid Kit should contain supplies necessary to tend to a variety of injuries. Pack a First Aid Kit in each of your emergency kits. For Grab and Go Kits, a small First Aid Kit is sufficient but it's a good idea to include a larger, well stocked First Aid Kit in your Home Kit. Do not forget about your pets; you may need to treat their injuries as well.

TASK #11: Make sure you have a First Aid Kit in all of your Emergency Kits.

1. Purchase First Aid Kits for each of your emergency kits from your local drug store or emergency preparedness store.

2. Check with your local community to find out who offers first aid courses; sign up. Knowing what to do could help save a life.

Work Kits

Nobody knows where they will be when an earthquake strikes. Hopefully, it will take place in the middle of the night when we are safely tucked into our beds. However, we need to be prepared in case we are away from home. Many of us spend many hours at the office – what if you were in your office when the ground starts shaking? What are your plans if you or a member of your family cannot immediately return home after the earthquake?

To be prepared - you need to keep a Work Grab and Go Kit at your place of business. Never underestimate the power of a good pair of walking shoes. Think about the shoes you wear to work. If you are like most of us, they are not designed for walking very far. You may have to walk down several flights of stairs to evacuate your building or hike a considerable distance to reach your destination.

In addition to walking shoes, ensure you have a light jacket, raincoat, or a poncho in your Work Kit. Do not forget your medications (check with your family doctor or pharmacy before storing any medications), money and your completed Out of Area Contact card – as you will want to connect with your family after a significant event when cell phones may not work.

Some businesses have emergency supplies in place for their employees, but employers cannot take into account your personal needs. It is your responsibility to ensure you have the supplies you need with you.

As a diabetic, I keep my medical supplies properly stored at my office in my personal Work Kit. I have thought through situations I could be faced with and have planned accordingly. What do you need to plan for?

TASK #12: Ensure you have a Work Kit stocked with supplies you will need until you can return home.

1. Purchase a backpack and assemble supplies you will need for your Work Kit.

2. Keep your work kit safely stored near your work station.

Grab and Go Kit Check List – Work Kit

Use items listed for the adult's Grab and Go Kit. Additional items to consider include:

☐ Walking shoes

☐ Jacket

☐ Maps/GPS – may or may not be working

☐ Compass

☐ Any other items you may require

Emergency Food

Many of us return home from work tired at the end of the day. We pop our dinner into the microwave and "poof" - three minutes later dinner is ready. Well, some of us still cook, but the same idea prevails. We rely on electricity or gas to cook our next meal, but an earthquake could interrupt the power supply. No electricity or gas – no cooking. So now what do you do? There are options available if you plan ahead.

First, ensure you have enough food on hand (in your Home Kit) to get you and your family through the event. When storing emergency food take into account your family's requirements. Consider special diets, allergies, and even certain likes or dislikes.

Canned foods work well. Remember to include that manual can opener in your Home Kit. There is nothing worse than having canned food in your kit with no way to open the cans. Canned soup, tuna, stews and even Alphagetti are handy. These menu items are probably not something you would serve for dinner tonight, but they will be useful if it is not possible to cook dinner in the usual way.

Fruit snacks, granola bars, and trail mix along with other packaged foods with a long shelf life are good options. These choices work well in your Grab and Go Kits as they are lighter to carry than canned foods. When selecting food, it is important to make choices that will not increase your thirst or require substantial quantities of water for preparation; tap water may not be available in the hours following an earthquake.

When planning food items, check with emergency preparedness and camping stores. These outlets carry a variety of ready-to-use foods. Some of these items are self-heating and have a five year shelf life.

If you have a barbeque, keep your propane tank at least half full. This will ensure you have a valuable source of cooking if the electricity is out. Never bring the barbecue inside your house or garage – it must always be used outside as fumes could seriously harm everyone in your house.

When the power is out consider the food you have in your refrigerator. Plan ahead of time which food you will remove from your refrigerator as food will stay colder longer if the door is not opened repeatedly. Every time you open the refrigerator door it loses cold air.

If you are not sure whether a food item is safe to eat do not take any chances. You may put yourself and your family at risk of illness from eating contaminated food. Following an earthquake, it may not be easy to see your family doctor. Do not take chances with food – if in doubt throw it out.

TASK #13: Ensure you have food for your family for at least seven days in your Home Kit.

1. Plan your family's meals for a minimum of seven days.

2. Purchase the required packaged and canned foods and store in your Home Kit.

3. Consider allergies or special requirements family members may have when selecting food for your Home Kit.

4. Be sure to include your pet's food requirements in your home kit.

	Food	Home Kit	Grab & Go Kit
1			
2			
3			
4			
5			
6			
7			
8			
9			
10			

Emergency Water

We cannot survive very long without water. All your kits need to contain enough water for you, your family and your pets. A calculation chart is provided to determine how much water your family will need for seven days.

Most people require at least 2 litres (2 quarts) of water each day for drinking, but if you live in a warmer climate the amount of water you need can be significantly more because your body requires water for cooling. Remember, additional water is needed for food preparation and hygiene. As a general rule of thumb, store at least 4 litres (1 gallon) of water per person, per day. If you have pets, allow one litre (one quart) per day for each average size dog or cat. Larger dogs will require more water. Check with your vet if you are unsure how much water your pet will require.

There are a number of ways you can store water to ensure you have enough. Select the method that works best for you and your family.

Bottled Water: An easy and convenient way to store water. Simply purchase bottled water from your grocery store. Use the chart to calculate how much water you and your family would need for seven days and purchase the required amount. When purchasing bottled water check the expiry dates. Sealed bottled water has a shelf life of two years. When the water gets close to the expiry date you and your family can drink it or it can be donated.

Refilling Water Bottles: Tap water works well if you prefer to refill your own bottles. Make sure your bottles are clean. Use plastic containers such as water, pop, soda or juice bottles with screw-on lids that fit tightly. Tap water stored in water bottles has a shelf life of six months. When using well water, check with your health department about proper storage.

Do not use plastic milk jugs to store water as it is difficult to remove protein and fat residues left in the jugs. Over time this can cause bacteria to grow and contaminate your water.

You can purchase water bottles designed to store water. Any containers you select to store water should be labeled as being suitable for food or beverage storage. Be cautious about using glass bottles as they could fall and break during an earthquake resulting in the loss of your water supply.

Freezing Water: This is a good option if you lose electricity; frozen water will help keep frozen food usable for a longer period of time. In addition, you will have a supply of cold water once thawed. When storing water in the freezer, leave 5-8 cm (2-3 inches) of air space in the top of the container before freezing. Without air space, the container could expand and break. Use only clean plastic bottles – not milk containers as discussed in Refilling Water Bottles.

Home Delivery: If you have water delivered to your home, calculate how much water your household will need for seven days and order extra bottles to meet your requirements. As you receive your ongoing deliveries rotate through the bottles so you always have fresh water on hand. This also works well in your office if you have water delivered.

Boiling Water: You may be asked by authorities to boil your tap water to ensure it is safe for drinking after an earthquake or major disaster. To boil water effectively, you must keep it at a full boil for at least one minute. At elevations over 2,000 meters (6,500 feet) you should boil water for at least two minutes to make it potable.

Bleach: After an earthquake, water can become contaminated and you may be required to purify water before drinking. Unscented household bleach with five percent chlorine can be used. When purifying water, keep it at room temperature and follow directions exactly as stated on the bleach bottle. DO NOT add a few extra drops of bleach just to make sure the water is going be safe to drink. By adding extra bleach you could put your family and pets at risk.

Water Purification Tablets: These tablets are available from emergency preparedness or camping stores and can be used to purify your water. Make sure you follow directions exactly as stated on the package.

Hot Water Tanks: I am often asked if water in your hot water tank is suitable for drinking. You need to be careful as sediments can gather in the tank making it dangerous to drink. I would suggest using bottled water just to be safe - however, water from your hot water tank can be used to wash your hands or dishes.

Water Storage: Store water in a cool, dry place away from direct sunlight. Keep it away from chemicals (such as weed killers or gasoline) because if chemical containers fall into your water supply it could be compromised. Water stored in bottles or jugs is heavy. Ensure that your storage shelf is strong enough to support the weight. Make sure your water bottles or jugs are secured so they cannot fall during an earthquake.

When the expiry date of your water draws near and the seal has not been broken, ask yourself if you have too much on hand for your family to drink? If so, you may be able to donate the water to charity. If, however, you have refilled water bottles with tap water, use it to water plants.

TASK #14: Ensure you have made provisions for enough water for you, your family and your pets for a minimum of seven days.

1. Select the best method for storing water for you and your family.

2. Use the chart provided to calculate how much water you need for seven days.

3. Find a location where you can safely store your water.

Amount of water required for my family

Calculate the amount of water needed by your family members for a single day then multiply it by seven. That is the total amount of water you need to store for use over seven days.

Step 1

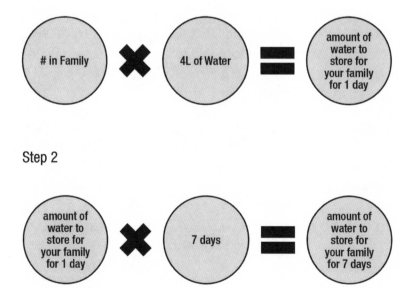

Step 2

Children and Disaster

I am often asked by parents if involving children in emergency planning will scare them. As a parent myself, I appreciate their concern, but the important question is – won't your children be even more frightened during an earthquake if they don't know what to do? I believe children need to be involved in developing your family emergency plan at an age appropriate level. Introducing children to concepts of emergency preparedness helps to keep them safe.

Having emergency plans in place and practicing your plans, ensures your children will feel confident because they know what to do. They will know how to connect with your family at your Family Meeting Place and what number to call to reach your Out of Area Contact if you are not together when disaster strikes.

In school, children practice fire drills; many schools participate in the annual Shake Out earthquake drill. This means that your children may already have a good concept of what to do when an earthquake strikes. Do not let the drills stop there - it is important to practice drills at home so your children will be prepared to act appropriately wherever they are. Assuming your children know what to do at home when a disaster strikes is not enough – you need to practice with them.

Ask your children's school and daycare operators what earthquake plans are in place. Learn what emergency supplies are stored on-site and how long your children will be able to stay at the facility if you are unable to pick them up. Make sure you provide the school and daycare with the name of someone you trust who can pick them up should you be unable to reach the facility. This person should be a friend, neighbour or family member who lives near your school and is willing to take on the responsibility.

While it is extremely tough to do, parents need to fight the urge to run to their children during an earthquake. You may put yourself at risk of being hit by falling or shooting debris, especially if your house has not been properly prepared. Wait until the shaking has stopped and then check your surroundings before leaving your safe place. Many injuries are sustained during an earthquake when people run to other locations within their homes. If you get injured during the earthquake you are not going to be much help to your kids.

Outlined in this guidebook are several steps you can take to ensure your home is prepared for an earthquake. Go through each room in your home with your children and identify the safe areas in an earthquake - under a desk for example or against an interior wall. Refer to the section "When the Earth Starts Moving" in this guide- book to learn what you and your family need to do the moment an earthquake strikes.

To help ease your concern during an earthquake, teach your children to sing a song when they **Drop, Cover and Hold On**. This accom- plishes two things – first, you will know your children are okay when you hear them sing, secondly, singing will help take your children's minds off the shaking. Once the shaking has stopped, check on your children. Go cautiously – watch for fallen debris and broken glass. At the same time, be aware of the possibility of aftershocks.

If you have young children who sleep in cribs, make sure their cribs are in a safe location away from windows. There should be nothing hanging on the wall near the crib that could fall when the earth starts moving.

If your children spend time with another parent in another home, it is important to ensure they have emergency plans and Grab and Go Kits at both locations. Use the same Out of Area Contact for both homes.

When my children were little, they alternated each week, spending time with me and with their dad. I made sure they had earthquake plans, family meeting places and Grab and Go Kits in both homes.

TASK #15: Take the necessary steps to ensure your kids are prepared for a disaster.

1. With your kids find the best place to **Drop, Cover and Hold On** in each room of your home.

2. Select a song that you and your children will sing in your safe spot during an earthquake.

3. Research emergency plans in place at your children's school and or daycare facility. Prepare Grab and Go Kits for your kids' daycare and school, if required.

4. If your children spend time with another parent or with grand-parents, ensure they are prepared at both homes.

Planning for your Kids

Earthquake Song:

School Name & Number:

Daycare Name & Number:

Neigbour who can pick up kids from school/daycare:

Seniors and People with Disabilities

As we age, we may not be able to do quite what we were able to do as younger folk. Over time our needs and our capabilities change. If we live with a disability we may have additional needs to consider when developing our emergency plans. The point is - everybody needs an emergency plan and everybody's emergency plan will be different.

If you are a senior or a person with a disability you will likely need to store additional items in your emergency kits to meet your needs. You might need help in putting your emergency plan together and making your home safe. Of course, this will depend on how active and able-bodied you are. You know your abilities better than anyone and you need to plan accordingly to ensure your preparedness.

Many of us will have medical needs to consider. It is important to talk with your health care professional to learn how your needs can best be addressed. Before storing medications, consult with experts. Have your pharmacist print out a list of medications you take. Keep a copy of your medications with your health insurance records in your Grab and Go Kit. One of the most common themes we find when responding to apartment fires is that people cannot remember what medications they are on or what dosage they take.

If you live in the same area as other family members make sure your name and number are included on their Out of Area Contact card. This will help you locate family members and learn their condition following an earthquake. It will also update your family members on your condition. Being in touch with family members will allow you to focus on what needs to be done next.

I was attending an event where I met a senior named Carole from New Zealand. Carole lives on her own in a house on the edge of town in a fairly remote area. Her daughter Lisa and son in law live in a different part of town and Carole was concerned how they would connect after a disaster. I explained the Out of Area Contact process to her and then agreed to be her Out of Area Contact.

Several months later, I was sitting at home when my phone rang – I answered the call and it was from Lisa, the daughter of Carole. Lisa explained they had just had an earthquake and she was not able to contact her mom. She was very worried as her mom lived on her own. I said I would make the call and see if I could connect with Carole.

The first two attempts were unsuccessful but on the third try my call went through and I had Carole on the line. You can only image the relief Carole felt when I was able to tell her that Lisa, her son in law and grandchildren were all fine and had suffered minimal damage from the earthquake. Carole had been worried sick when she could not contact them. Now that she knew her family was OK she was able to concentrate on dealing with the aftermath of the earthquake.

If you need help with your planning, a trusted neighbour may be able to help you develop your plan and provide assistance in an emergency. If you attend a club or church group, use these contacts as part of your network and let trusted people know what your needs are so they may be able to help you during times of disaster. You may ask one of them to check on you should something happen in your building or neighbourhood.

When putting together your emergency kit, refer to the section on emergency kits and jot down the items you will need to include. If you rely on an electric wheelchair and the battery goes dead, you have a problem. Think about that situation now – and identify how this can be handled?

> *At a seminar I was conducting, an older gentleman who relied on a walking cane kept an umbrella by his front door - if he were not able to find his cane, the umbrella could double as a walking cane. Sometimes we need to be creative in solving problems.*

If you have mobility problems, identify methods you could use to evacuate your building. During building evacuations, you may not be able to use the elevators, so plan for this possibility. In advance, ask a neighbour to check on you and notify the fire department that you are in your apartment. If necessary, wave a towel from your balcony or window so you will be noticed. Check to see if your building has a refuge area. This is a safe area that has been pre-identified. The Fire Department would know to check this area.

With emergency planning there is never one right solution – it is about having plans for a variety of responses so when the emergency occurs you will be able to do the best you can with what you have. Identify your strengths and weaknesses and plan accordingly. We all need to have our emergency plans in place with a number of options available to us.

TASK 16: Identify what you, older family members or people with disabilities may need to consider following an emergency or disaster - for example, purchase an extra walking stick.

	Tasks to Complete
1	Have your pharmacist print out your meds and dosage
2	Talk to a neighbor who will help you during a disaster
3	
4	
5	
6	
7	
8	
9	
10	

Pets and Disaster

Pets are important members of our family. We think of them as our kids. When I present emergency preparedness sessions, I can always tell who the pet owners are - when I introduce the Pet Section, pet owners perk up while those who do not own pets roll their eyes and wonder what I am going to say next.

If you do not own a pet, you can skip this section. But for pet owners, this is an important part of a family's emergency plan. Disasters that impact us will also affect our pets.

In 2005, millions watched as Hurricane Katrina ripped through Louisiana and other states destroying homes and turning the lives of the residents upside down. Thousands of people were told to evacuate but many refused to leave because they could not take their pets with them. Sadly, people and pets lost their lives.

While you are encouraged to take your pets with you, evacuating with animals is not as simple as it sounds. Sometimes frightened pets hide. If evacuating because of a house fire you may only have seconds to get out and will not have time to search for pets. With other events you may have more time, but if your pet is hiding, you could be faced with a tough decision because your personal safety must take priority.

When the urgency to evacuate isn't as pressing, it's important to leave with your pet. If you take a few simple steps in advance, you can ensure both you and your pets will be prepared to evacuate when the time comes.

The first step is to develop a pet Grab and Go Kit. Like Grab and Go Kits packed for family members, your pet's kit will include items they require during a period of disruption. When evacuating, you will grab your Grab and Go Kit and your pet's as you head out the door. A list of the contents for your pet's Grab and Go Kit is included at the end of this section.

> *A story from British Columbia's 2003 firestorm has stayed with me. A family was told to evacuate their home due to the fast approaching forest fire. During a previous evacuation a few years back, they had been away from home for only a night so they expected to repeat their short-term evacuation experience again this time. Rather than taking their dog with them, they decided it would be better to leave him in his dog run where he had shelter, plenty of food and water. During the night the fire changed direction and roared through their property. Sadly, their dog did not survive. The family was devastated. They had truly believed they were doing what was best for their dog but everything went terribly wrong.*

As pet lovers, our hearts go out to what this family lived through. Do not let this happen to you. As you plan, identify what you and your pets could be faced with, then prepare to meet those possibilities.

Planning a destination for pets is crucial. You must choose a location that welcomes pets whether it is the home of a friend or relative, a pet-friendly hotel, or a boarding kennel.

If for any reason you must leave your pets behind, post a notice on your front and back doors to notify searchers that animals are on your property. Do not leave them tied up or locked in a room of your house. Give them free run of your home.

Often in emergency situations, evacuation centers open to provide evacuees with a safe place to stay. Since learning the lessons of Hurricane Katrina, a greater number of evacuation centers welcome pets. However, do not assume you will be able to keep your pet with you at an evacuation center – most likely pets will be placed in a designated area of the center. Check with your local city hall to learn what plans are in place for disaster-displaced pets.

Transporting your pet is another consideration. Will your pet freely go into his carrier or will this be a challenge?

> *Sophie my cat and I have a fighting match every time I bring out the carrier. As soon as she sees it, she hisses and spits and extends her claws to their full length. She immediately "evacuates" the room and runs to her favorite hiding spot.*

> *Fast forward to an emergency situation -- the stress experienced by both Sophie and me will make the situation challenging. I need to plan in advance how I will evacuate with my cat before an earthquake strikes. My veterinarian suggested that I keep a pillowcase in her Grab and Go Kit as it may be less stressful for Sophie to "stuff" her into a pillowcase than try to stuff her into the pet carrier.*

If you own a large dog too heavy to carry, it may not be practical to use a kennel for transporting him. Keep a leash in your Grab and Go Kit because both you and your dog might end up walking. In addition to a leash, consider packing booties to fit over paws as there may be debris on streets and sidewalks.

Identifying a "Pet Buddy" is the next step in developing your pet emergency plan. A Pet Buddy is someone you trust and who is willing to care for your pet during an emergency. If you have a "dog walker" they often make good Pet Buddies.

In the Family Photo section we noted the importance of having a photo of your pet alone as well as one of your pet with your family. Should the need arise, these photos will allow you to prove that you and your pet belong to each other.

Register your dog with your local animal control. This will increase the odds of your dog being returned to you if you become separated. Animal control shelters routinely receive unlicensed dogs making it difficult to track their owners. Ensure that your dog wears a collar with its license and your contact information attached. If you are evacuated, record your temporary contact information and attach to your pet's collar. Microchips and tattoos help to track a missing pet. Ask your vet if this is something you should consider.

Once back home after an evacuation, keep a close eye on your pet. Take the same steps you would if you had moved into a new home. Keep your pet indoors until they are accustomed to their surroundings. You should also go outside with them until they are once again familiar with your home's exterior surroundings. Disasters are as stressful for pets as they are for us. If you have concerns, check with your veterinarian.

If your pet is an animal other than a dog or cat, plan appropriate emergency supplies specific to their needs.

TASK #17: Complete the following steps to ensure your pets are prepared to evacuate when necessary.

1. Prepare a Grab and Go Kit for each pet with the items they will require.

2. Identify "Pet Friendly" locations where you could evacuate with your family and pet.

3. Find a "Pet Buddy," someone you can rely on to look after your pet if you are not at home.

4. Register your dog with your local Animal Control.

5. Take a photo of your pet alone and a photo of you with your pet.

Grab and Go Kit Check List – Pet Kit

Consider the following items for your Dog and Cat (or turtle's) Grab and Go Kit. Add additional items specific to your pet's needs. If your pet is not a dog or cat, ensure you have the supplies they will need.

Pet Grab and Go Kit (Dogs & Cats)

☐ Photo of your pet

☐ Photo of you and your pet

☐ Veterinarian and Vaccination records kept in a zip locked bag

☐ Medication Chart – listing medications, dose and frequency

☐ Water

☐ Plastic bags for waste disposal

☐ First Aid Kit

☐ Paper towels

- ☐ Medications (Check with veterinarian for proper storage)
- ☐ Newspapers
- ☐ Veterinarian and pharmacy contact info
- ☐ Blanket
- ☐ Food – wet food is better as it will not increase thirst
- ☐ Toys
- ☐ Can opener
- ☐ Treats
- ☐ Non spill food and water bowls
- ☐ Feeding Schedule
- ☐ Other items your pet may require

Dog Grab and Go Kit

- ☐ Leash and muzzle
- ☐ Waterproof pouch that can attach to the collar with identification information inside
- ☐ Masking Tape for collar to write new address
- ☐ Other items your dog may require

Cat Grab and Go Kit

- ☐ Non clumping cat litter
- ☐ Travel Bag or pillow case for transporting
- ☐ Other items your cat may require

Planning for your Pets

Vet Address:

Vet Phone:

Pet Buddy:

Pet Friendly Hotel:

When the Earth Starts Moving

Now it is time to learn and practice what to do when the earth starts moving. In North America **Drop, Cover and Hold On** is the action to take during an earthquake. You and your family members must practice **Drop, Cover and Hold On** until it becomes second nature.

courtesy of Earthquake Country Alliance www.earthquakecountry.org

Drop down onto your hands and knees. This protects you from falling while allowing you to move if you need to.

Cover your head and neck (ideally your whole body) under a sturdy table or desk. If there is nothing to crawl under, drop near an inside corner of the building and cover your head and face. Do not try and run into another room just to get to a table.

Hold On until the shaking stops. Be warned and be prepared - your heavy table or desk could move around the room.

Drop, Cover and Hold On will help protect you and your family from falling and flying debris. It will also help protect you from non-structural hazards and increase the chance of your ending up in a survivable space should the building be damaged. The space under a sturdy table or desk is likely to remain somewhat intact even if the building is damaged. We have seen news stories from around the world showing tables and desks still standing with rubble all around them.

With your family, go through each room of your home and find your safe locations. Practice **Drop, Cover and Hold On** until it becomes second nature. Do not position yourselves near windows, large appliances, walls with heavy pictures or objects that could fall and injure you and your family.

Many communities around the world participate in the **Great ShakeOut,** annual earthquake drill. This drill provides an excellent opportunity for your family, neighbours and co-workers to practice **Drop, Cover and Hold On**. Visit their website at www.shakeoutbc. ca and register for this drill that takes place each October. From this site you can link to other Shakeout sites throughout the world.

What to do during an Earthquake

You don't know where you will be when the earthquake happens, so you need to think about a variety of locations you could be in and identify what your best response to the earthquake would be. If you are **in bed** when an earthquake strikes, stay in bed, hold on and cover your head with a pillow and wait for the shaking to stop. If you stay in bed your chance of being injured is much less. When the shaking stops, get out of bed carefully. Use the shoes stored under your bed to protect your feet from broken glass if you need to go to another location in your home.

If you are in a high-rise – the same drill applies – **Drop, Cover and Hold On**. Move away from windows. Never use the elevators. Be aware that the fire alarm or sprinkler system may turn on during an earthquake.

I am often asked what should you do if an earthquake strikes when you are not at home?

If you are outside, it is still **Drop, Cover and Hold On**. During the New Zealand earthquake, debris fell off buildings and landed on the sidewalks. Had you been on the sidewalk you would likely have suffered serious injury. Move away from buildings, power lines, trees, signs, cars and other hazards.

If you are in your car, pull over to the side of the road and turn off your engine. Avoid parking on or near overpasses, bridges, signs, or power lines. Stay in your car until the shaking stops. Listen to your car radio to learn of road closures. Do not get out of your car if there are downed power lines on or near your car – wait for help to arrive.

If you are on a bus stay in your seat until the bus stops and the shaking has stopped. Take cover in a crouched position and protect your head from falling or shooting debris.

If you and your family are in a theatre or stadium, stay in your seat and protect your head and neck with your arms. Do not try to leave your seat until the shaking has stopped. If evacuating after the earthquake, walk slowly. Watch for anything that has fallen or that could fall on you.

If you are on the beach – again it is **Drop, Cover and Hold On**. If there is nothing to hold onto, put one arm over your head and use the other arm to brace yourself until the shaking stops. Next, move to higher ground as water levels could rise. Listen to your radio for tsunami warnings. If you are in an area that could be affected by a tsunami, move inland three km (two miles). If you are in a high traffic area, you might reach your destination faster if you walk or bike rather than using your car.

When an earthquake occurs, people often get the urge to run outside. Imagine what could have happened to you and your family members had you run outside during the New Zealand earthquake where sidewalks were covered in debris. Studies have shown that most earthquake injuries take place while people are changing locations inside their home or running outside or running to the inside of their home if they are outside.

Many of us were taught in school to find a doorway and brace yourself in the door frame. People are now being warned that a door frame is not a safe place. In a door frame you open yourself up to the possibility of flying debris coming at you from two directions. You also run the risk of the door slamming shut against your fingers – and we know the pain that can cause.

Every time a major earthquake strikes, an email entitled the **Triangle of Life** resurfaces. This email provides an alternative to **Drop, Cover and Hold On**. What the email suggests you do will put you and your family in great danger. In Canada and the United States we do not promote the Triangle of Life. If you visit www.myeqplan.ca you can read more on the Triangle of Life.

When presenting sessions on earthquake preparedness, I am often asked - will my house be damaged when an earthquake strikes? Will my family be injured if they stay in the house during the earthquake? Will I be able to stay in my home after an earthquake? And the list of questions goes on and on.

These are difficult questions to answer. There are so many variables that come into play when an earthquake strikes. Some of these are:

What have you and your family done to make your home safe? Is your house secured to its foundation? What supplies have you prepared in advance? Does your family practice **Drop, Cover and Hold On** when an earthquake strikes?

How you answer these questions and the steps you have taken to prepare in advance will determine how well you and your family will survive the earthquake.

With so many variables around the location of an earthquake and the condition of your house, it's easy to understand why no one can predict what will happen to your home, but we do know this: If you are prepared and have taken the necessary steps to make your home safe and if you **Drop, Cover and Hold On** during an earthquake your odds of survival greatly increase.

Remember – most injuries caused by an earthquake take place when people run from room to room inside their home or run outside, or if they are outside they try to run inside. Make sure you and your family members know to immediately **Drop, Cover and Hold On** when faced with an earthquake.

TASK #18: Make sure you and your family members know what to do when an earthquake strikes. This needs to become second nature to all of us.

1. Practice **Drop, Cover and Hold On** until it becomes second nature.

2. Register for your local shake out drill www.shakeoutbc.ca

3. Find safe places in each room of your home where you and your family can take cover when an earthquake strikes. Record these locations in the chart below.

	Room	Safe Place
1		
2		
3		
4		
5		
6		
7		
8		
9		
10		

What to do After the Earthquake

Once the shaking has stopped there are a number of things around your home you will need to check. First, view your immediate surroundings before leaving your safe spot (under a heavy table or against an interior wall). If your home has been well prepared there will likely be minimal debris, but if your home has not been made safe, debris could be a challenge. You might be faced with broken glass, toppled furniture, or broken dishes just to mention a few.

Your top priority will be the safety of your family and pets. Ensure they are all safe, then check to see if there is structural damage to your home. The result of these checks will determine your next move.

If your family and pets are safe and your home is structurally sound, listen to the radio to get updates on the earthquake. If your power is out, use the radio from your Grab and Go Kit or Home Kit. These reports will provide information about the extent of damage in your community.

Evacuation centers will open as soon as possible, but that could take 72 hours or longer. Call your Out of Area Contact if you are unable to connect with family members. If family members are at work they should enact emergency plans you developed relating to the workplace.

If your home has not suffered any major damage, it may not be necessary to evacuate. In that case, retrieve your Home Kit and set up camp in your home. This is when you realize the value of having emergency plans and supplies in place before the earthquake strikes.

TASK #19: **Identify what you need to check inside and outside your home following an earthquake e.g. broken glass, gas lines to appliances and power lines and list in the chart below.**

	Things to check after an earthquake in our home
1	
2	
3	
4	
5	
6	
7	
8	
9	
10	

Evacuating your Home

How to evacuate your home is something to consider in advance. Evacuations are necessary for a variety of reasons. If your home is obviously unsafe after an earthquake or if you are ordered to evacuate, you have no choice. If you are not required to evacuate and are able to remain in your home, you will be thankful to have emergency plans and supplies in place. None of us like to think this could be a reality, but if you ask people who have been evacuated – they too thought it would never happen to them. Famous last words.

When facing an evacuation, you will need to answer three questions. If you have prepared in advance you will easily be able to answer them.

1. Where will you, your family and pets go?

2. Who can take you, your family and your pets?

3. What do you need to take with you?

Addressing these three questions in advance will ease the evacuation process and save considerable time.

If you have insurance you will be much better off. Make certain you have adequate insurance coverage. If you live in an earthquake-prone area, consult with your insurance broker regarding appropriate coverage. Don`t ever assume you are insured for something – clarify this with your agent before the disaster strikes.

With appropriate coverage in place, insurance will cover some costs incurred by you and your family. In responding to emergencies within the City of Vancouver, time and time again I see people become homeless simply because they did not purchase insurance or they did not purchase adequate insurance.

If you evacuate your home because it is unsafe to stay, you need to have predetermined locations to reconnect with your family. When you developed your Family Meeting Places you identified potential locations where you and your family could reconnect. If you identified friends or family who will let you stay with them, this is the time to accept their offer. You will need to check and see if they have also been impacted by the earthquake.

Most communities will open Evacuation Centers to look after those who have been displaced. In an earthquake, these centers could take several days to open as they need to be found safe by a building inspector. Your community does not want to open a center only to learn it was damaged. If there were aftershocks additional damage could occur putting everyone at risk.

Following disasters other than earthquakes you will not likely have to wait for evacuation centers to open. However, it is still important to be prepared to look after yourself and family for at least a week. In the aftermath of Super Storm Sandy and Hurricane Katrina in the USA and the earthquakes in New Zealand, we learned that it takes time to get resources to people. Keep this in mind when completing your Family Emergency Plan.

TASK #20: Ensure you and your family have plans in place in the event you have to evacuate

1. Identify family or friends you, your family and pets could stay with if evacuated.

2. Identify hotels (pet friendly if you have pets) that may be able to take you and your family.

	Where we can stay if evacuated (Name - Address - Phone)
1	
2	
3	
4	
5	

Update and Practice Your Plan

Disaster planning does not stop with the development of a plan and purchasing your supplies. An important piece of the puzzle is to make sure your plan is kept current. You do not want to call your Out of Area Contact to find their phone number changed several months ago, or to learn after the earthquake that your medications, food and water expired last month or the batteries for your flashlight and radio no longer work.

Form the habit of maintaining emergency supplies you, your family and pets will rely on during a disaster. This includes changing batteries in your smoke and carbon monoxide alarms, updating emergency supplies, confirming your Out of Area Contact number, and asking your pet buddy if they are still available to help with your pets. You need to make sure that anything you rely on during an emergency or disaster is current.

An ideal time to do this is when the clocks change. If you get into the habit of reviewing your emergency plan twice a year, you will know that your emergency supplies will be ready when disaster strikes.

TASK #21: Use the chart below to record the expiry date of all your emergency supplies.

1. Complete the chart below to ensure you know what items need to be replaced before the expiry date (batteries, first aid supplies, medications, food, and water).

2. On your calendar mark "Update Emergency Supplies" as a reminder to update your plans and supplies each spring and fall when the clocks change. Remove and replace expired items.

3. Conduct exercises twice a year when the clocks change – this will ensure you and your family know what to do when disaster strikes.

	Items with an Expiry Date	Expiry Date
1		
2		
3		
4		
5		
6		
7		

Summary

A great deal of information is covered in the pages of this guidebook. Acting on this information will help you and your family members develop an emergency plan without having to rifle through millions of pages on the web. If you have not done so already, take action and work through this guidebook to put your family emergency plans in place.

The time to plan and prepare is now, before disaster strikes. Once the earthquake hits, it will be too late.

Remember - the hardest thing about not having an emergency plan in place is trying to explain to your family why you failed to prepare.

Exercise #1
Home Evacuation Routes

Purpose: To test the evacuation routes from each room in your home so you and your family will be comfortable and familiar with the process to evacuate from your home during an emergency or disaster.

Supplies: Graph paper, black and red felt pens, ruler

Instructions:

1. Read through each step to ensure you understand how the exercise works.

2. Gather the supplies you need to complete the exercise.

3. Use graph paper and a black felt pen to draw the floor plan of your home. Use a separate piece of paper for each floor of your home. To draw to scale, use one square for each square foot of your home. Don't be afraid to estimate if you are not sure of the exact dimensions of your home.

4. Mark the location of all doorways and windows on the floor plan and include your family meeting place on this plan.

5. With your family go into each room of your house. Identify two (if possible) evacuation routes from each room that lead to your family meeting place across the street. The evacuation route

Exercises

The following exercises provide scenarios designed to test your family's emergency plans. They will identify any gaps you may have in your plans. Like everything else the time to exercise your plans is now, before the disaster strikes.

Work through each exercise with your family to get them familiar with the process they will follow when an emergency or disaster strikes. When the exercise is completed take the necessary steps to fix any gaps identified in your plans to ensure you and your family are ready for whatever comes your way.

Before starting the exercises - read through the exercise and gat the supplies you will need. Do not skip any steps – you want to m sure your emergency plans will get you and your family through disaster you may be faced with.

Remember: Practice make perfect.

could be through either a door or a window.

6. Practice evacuating from each room of your home and gathering at your family meeting place. Once all family members are comfortable with evacuating from each room, use the red felt pen to mark the route on your floor plan. Use common sense to determine whether or not someone should go out the window during the exercise – you do not want to unnecessarily increase personal danger. However, in an emergency leaving through a window could be a sensible option.

7. Once evacuation routes are marked in red, have each family member go to a room in your house and perform an activity they would normally carry out in that room. Activities might include doing homework, watching TV, or making cookies.

8. Set off your smoke alarm. Instruct your family to evacuate the house and meet at your family meeting place. This will identify how familiar each family member is with your evacuation plan.

9. If you have pets, discuss how you will evacuate each pet. Stress to family members that personal safety is everyone's first priority. Never put yourself in danger as many people have been injured while trying to save their pets.

10. Have family members who plan to leave through the door nearest the Grab and Go Kits take as many kits as they can.

11. Address any issues that become obvious while practicing the evacuation of your home. If necessary, make changes to your evacuation plan.

12. As part of your home evacuation practice, set off your smoke alarm in the middle of the night without informing your family. This will identify how successful your family will be in a real-life evacuation.

Debrief: Afterwards, discuss the evacuation exercise with your family.

1. Review each section of the exercise and allow family members to comment on how well the process worked. Note their feelings. Was anyone fearful? Were they comfortable with the procedure? Do not make light of their feelings – you want everyone to feel confident carrying out an evacuation that could save their lives.

2. If necessary, update your emergency plan using information you collected during your family debrief.

3. Test your evacuation plan twice a year. A good time to review the plan is when the clocks change.

	What do we need to update in our Emergency Plan
1	
2	
3	
4	
5	
6	
7	
8	
9	
10	

Exercise #2
Utilities Identification

Purpose: This exercise will help familiarize family members with the location of utilities and safety equipment in your home and will teach them how to turn these utilities off when required.

Supplies: Floor plan from Exercise #1, green or blue felt pens, tags for noting instructions and attaching to utilities.

Instructions:

1. Use the floor plan created in Exercise #1 to identify and mark the location of utilities in your home. These may include but are not limited to:

   · gas meter

   · hot water tank

   · furnace

   · electrical panel

   · water shut off valve

   · fire extinguisher

   · smoke alarm

   · carbon monoxide alarm

   · well and/or pump

   · hot tub

   · swimming pool

   · other _____

   · other _____

   · other _____

2. With your family, review how and when to shut off the utilities in your home. If you have tenants or boarders, include them in this process if appropriate.

3. Stress the importance of your gas meter and remind family members to turn off the gas **only if they smell gas or hear the hissing sound natural gas makes**. Remember – never put yourself in danger. Personal safety always comes first.

4. Tag each utility with a description or diagram explaining how and when to turn it off. Refer to the owner's user manual or utility website to ensure shut-off information is accurate.

Exercise #3
What If…

Purpose: Nobody knows where they will be when the earthquake takes place. This makes it necessary to ensure that you and family members know how to **Drop, Cover and Hold On** wherever you are.

Your chances of survival will significantly increase when you **Drop, Cover and Hold On** in an earthquake. You need to practice this until it becomes second nature.

The "What If" exercise will help ensure your family takes the proper action during an earthquake, wherever they may be.

Instructions:

1. As you go about your daily routines, ask your family members, "If there were an earthquake right now what would you do?"

2. Ask each family member to describe the first steps they would take. "**Drop, Cover and Hold On**" is the answer you want to hear.

3. As you practice this exercise, family members will become familiar with assessing their surroundings and making informed decisions on where they can most safely **Drop, Cover and Hold On**.

It might be under a table, against an interior wall, or right where they are standing - with head protected. Remember, most injuries occur when people are running inside or outside their house or running from room to room.

Be sure you make the right decision when the earthquake strikes. **Drop, Cover and Hold On.**

About the Author

What would you do if a catastrophic event disrupted your life? Jackie Kloosterboer considers this question every day. She is a firm believer that we are all in this together, but worries that each of us may be on our own for several days – maybe even weeks. As a result, she makes it a practice to help families and businesses pull together resources and plans to mitigate losses and help prevent the loss of lives. Jackie hopes that the information in the book will help provide people with the tools to gather together their own supplies and help them be prepared to face whatever comes their way. The cornerstone of her philosophy is that those who are prepared will better survive whatever life throws at them.

You may contact Jackie to speak at your club, meeting or conference at:

myeqplan.com
myeqplan@gmail.com
or 604.355.2414